1,000,000 Books

are available to read at

---◆---

www.ForgottenBooks.com

---◆---

Read online
Download PDF
Purchase in print

ISBN 978-0-428-14962-8
PIBN 11249771

This book is a reproduction of an important historical work. Forgotten Books uses state-of-the-art technology to digitally reconstruct the work, preserving the original format whilst repairing imperfections present in the aged copy. In rare cases, an imperfection in the original, such as a blemish or missing page, may be replicated in our edition. We do, however, repair the vast majority of imperfections successfully; any imperfections that remain are intentionally left to preserve the state of such historical works.

Forgotten Books is a registered trademark of FB &c Ltd.
Copyright © 2018 FB &c Ltd.
FB &c Ltd, Dalton House, 60 Windsor Avenue, London, SW19 2RR.
Company number 08720141. Registered in England and Wales.

For support please visit www.forgottenbooks.com

1 MONTH OF
FREE
READING

at
www.ForgottenBooks.com

By purchasing this book you are eligible for one month membership to ForgottenBooks.com, giving you unlimited access to our entire collection of over 1,000,000 titles via our web site and mobile apps.

To claim your free month visit:

www.forgottenbooks.com/free1249771

* Offer is valid for 45 days from date of purchase. Terms and conditions apply.

English
Français
Deutsche
Italiano
Español
Português

www.forgottenbooks.com

Mythology Photography **Fiction**
Fishing Christianity **Art** Cooking
Essays Buddhism Freemasonry
Medicine **Biology** Music **Ancient**
Egypt Evolution Carpentry Physics
Dance Geology **Mathematics** Fitness
Shakespeare **Folklore** Yoga Marketing
Confidence Immortality Biographies
Poetry **Psychology** Witchcraft
Electronics Chemistry History **Law**
Accounting **Philosophy** Anthropology
Alchemy Drama Quantum Mechanics
Atheism Sexual Health **Ancient History**
Entrepreneurship Languages Sport
Paleontology Needlework Islam
Metaphysics Investment Archaeology
Parenting Statistics Criminology
Motivational

BULLETIN

OF THE

University of New Mexico

WHOLE NO. 87

CATALOGUE SERIES   APRIL 1917   VOLUME 30, No. 2

NEW MEXICO
INTERSCHOLASTIC MEET
MAY 3, 4, 5, 1917

ALBUQUERQUE, NEW MEXICO

PUBLISHED QUARTERLY BY THE UNIVERSITY OF NEW MEXICO
ENTERED MAY 1, 1906, AT ALBUQUERQUE, N. M. AS SECOND CLASS MATTER

D. of D.
MAY 5 1917

LC Control Number

2008   461873

Contents.

The New Mexico Interscholastic Meet.

In 1913 the authorities of the University, feeling that one of the great needs of the High Schools of the State was an opportunity to meet, at least once a year, in athletic and other contests, organized the University of New Mexico Track Athletic Association. A track meet was held in the spring of that year, at Albuquerque, and two high schools, Santa Fe and Albuquerque, contested for the banner. Although the beginning was small, a great deal of interest was aroused, and seven high schools took part in the next meet, when the Spalding Trophy was offered for the first time. Since that time the number of contesting schools has grown steadily. At the time of the meeting of the Educational Association in Albuquerque in November, 1915, the New Mexico High School Athletic Association was formed, and the 1916 meet was held under the joint auspices of this Association and the University. A new feature, the Basketball Tournament, was added, and in other ways the meet was the most successful of the series. The yearly meeting has done a great deal toward the unification of athletic standards in the state, and in bringing the high schools into closer and more cordial relationships.

At the annual business meeting of the N. M. High School Athletic Association, held at Santa Fe, November 29, 1916, an agreement was made whereby the Athletic and Oratorical Associations of the High

Schools were united under one set of officers, the name of the organization changed to "The New Mexico High School Athletic and Lyceum Association." Accordingly, the scope of the coming meet is to be enlarged to include oratorical and declamatory contests. This is bound to lead to a greater growth and a greater service, as both sides of student activity are now to be ·represented. The officers of the Association and the members of the University hope that every section of the state will be represented in all departments of the meet.

Program.

Thursday, May 3, 1917.

2:00 P. M.—Preliminary Games—Basketball Tournament.

8:00 P. M.—Semi-Final Games—Basketball Tournament.

Friday, May 4, 1917.

2:00 P. M.—Preliminary Events—Track and Field Meet.

8:00 P. M.—Final Championship Games — Basketball Tournament.

Saturday, May 5, 1917.

*10:00 A. M.—Declamatory Contest.

2:00 P. M.—Final Events—Track and Field Meet.

6:30 P. M.—Dinner and Presentation of Prizes.

*8:00 P. M.—Oratorical Contest.

---

*If considered advisable on account of the number of contestants, both contests may be held at either 10:00 A. M. or 8:00 P. M.

General Information.

Eligibility.

All matters of eligibility of teams or of individuals will be decided by the Board of Control of the New Mexico High School Athletic and Lyceum Association, according to the rules of that body, as given in the constitution. This applies to all contests.

Entries.

All entries must be made on the official entry blanks as sent out by the meet committee, properly filled out and signed by the Principal or Superintendent. These entry blanks must be returned to the committee on or before Tuesday, April 24. In the case of the Oratorical and Declamatory Contest the entries must also be accompanied by a statement from the Secretary of the section to the effect that the entrant was either first or second in the sectional contest. In case there has been no sectional contest, in any section, not more than one contestant for the prize in oratory and one contestant for the prize in declamation may be entered from that section.

Officials.

The officials of the Track Meet and Basketball Tournament will be chosen by the local committees. Any High School wishing to protest against any official may do so by filing written objection before the contest. No school may thus protest more than two officials.

Contestants to be Guests of the University.

All contestants will be guests of the University during the meet. Sleeping quarters will be provided in the University dormitories and elsewhere, and meals will be served in the University Dining Hall. Each contestant will receive a meal ticket entitling him to meals at the University Dining Hall Thursday noon to Sunday morning, inclusive. Meals taken before or after the above dates will be charged for at the regular rates.

Award of Prizes.

The cups, banners, and medals for the athletic events will be awarded at a dinner Saturday evening. The prizes for the Oratorical and Declamatory contests will be awarded after the contests.

Railway Rates.

The railways have granted a special rate of one and one-third round trip fares for this event, providing fifty tickets are sold. There should be many more than this. In buying your tickets to Albuquerque pay the regular one-way fare and obtain from the agent a ''receipt-certificate.'' This receipt-certificate must then be signed by Mr. A. O. Weese, of the University. You will then be allowed to purchase a ticket from Albuquerque to your home town for one-third regular fare. This rate is not limited to those taking part in the meet, but any others coming to Albuquerque at that time may avail themselves of this reduced rate, if the receipts are presented to Mr. Weese for validation. Tickets will be on sale May 1-5 inclusive; and are good for return until May 7.

Street Car Service.

Contestants arriving in Albuquerque should go directly to the University, where accommodations will be provided. Take the street car marked "University." There is a regular twelve-minute service on this line from 7:30 A. M. to 10:30 P. M.

Medals and Prizes.

Offered to Contestants in the Annual
Interscholastic Meet.

I.—The Track Meet.

The Spalding Trophy—This cup will become the permanent property of the High School which shall first win the meet three times. The cup is at present in the possession of Albuquerque High School, winners of the 1916 meet. This cup has been won twice by Roswell High School and once by Albuquerque High School.

Individual Medals for Each Event—Gold for first place, silver for second place, and bronze for third place, to become the property of the contestants earning them.

The Relay Cup—This cup will become the permanent property of the school winning the relay race.

The Championship Banner—This banner is awarded to the school winning the Track Meet.

II.—The Basketball Tournament.

The Championship Cup—This cup will become the permanent property of the school winning the Basketball Tournament.

III.—The Oratorical and Declamatory Contests.

Individual Medals—Gold for first place, silver for second place, and bronze for third place, for each contest. These medals are to be the property of the contestants winning them.

Note.—All members of the New Mexico High School Athletic and Lyceum Association are eligible to enter teams or individuals in any of the contests of the meet, but cups and banners will be awarded only to those schools whose support is derived principally from local taxation.

The Track and Field Meet.

Rule I.

1. The Banner shall be awarded to that High School each year which shall be declared winner of the annual meet.

2. The cup shall be awarded to that High School which shall first win the annual field meet three times, excluding ties. Each High School which wins the cup one year will have its name engraved on the cup and will retain it for that year.

Rule II.

1. That High School shall be champion which shall score a plurality of points.

2. Points shall be counted as follows:

A first place shall count five points.

A second place shall count three points.

A third place shall count two points.

In case of a tie the points shall be divided.

Rule III.

All disputes in regard to the possession of the cup shall be referred to the Board of Control.

Rule IV.

The number and order of events shall be as follows:

1. 100-yards run.
2. Putting 12-pound shot.
3. Half-mile run.
4. Pole vault.

5. 120-yards hurdle.
6. Running high jump.
7. 440-yards run.
8. Running broad jump.
9. 220-yards hurdle.
10. Running hop, step, and jump.
11. 220-yards run.
12. 1-mile run.
13. One-mile relay race, between teams of four men, each man to run ¼ mile.

Rule V.

Any High School which is a member of the Association may enter a team in this meet. No preliminary sectional contests are required.

Rule VI.

No High School shall enter a team of more than fourteen (14) men. Nor shall more than three (3) men be entered for any one event from any High School.

Rule VII.

Any competitor may enter as many events as he may desire.

Rule VIII.

All entries must be made on the official entry blanks as sent out by the meet committee, properly filled out and signed by the principal or superintendent. These entry blanks must be returned to the committee on or before Tuesday, April 24.

Rules for Track and Field Events.

I.—Officers.

The officers of the Interscholastic Meet shall be:
  One Referee.
  Four Inspectors to assist Referee.
  One Scorer.
  Five Assistant Scorers.
  One Clerk of the Course.
  Five Assistant Clerks of the Course.
  One Reporter.
  One Announcer, with Assistant, if necessary.
1. For Track Events:
     Four Judges at the Finish.
     Three Time-Keepers.
     One Starter.
2. For Field Events:
     Six Field Judges or Measurers.

II.—Referee.

The Referee shall, when appealed to, decide all questions whose settlement is not otherwise provided for in these rules. His decision shall be final and without appeal.

In case a race has been drawn into heats, and no more contestants appear than enough to make one heat, the Referee shall be empowered to see that the race is run in one heat; but in all races requiring more than one heat he shall see that no second man shall be debarred from a chance to qualify in the finals.

III.—Inspectors.

The Inspectors shall perform such duties as may be assigned to them by the Referee, and shall report

to him any violation of the rules which they observe
or are informed of.

IV.—Judges at the Finish.

Two Judges shall stand at one end of the tape, and
two at the other. One shall take the' winner, another
the second man, another the third man, and the other
the fourth. In case of disagreement the majority shall
decide. Their decision as to the order in which the
men finished shall be final and without appeal.

V.—Field Judges or Measurers.

The Field Judges shall measure, judge and record
each trial of each competitor in all games, whose record
is of distance or height. Their decision as to the per-
formance of each man shall be final and without appeal. There shall be six measurers: two for the hammer throwing and shot putting events, two for the
high jump and the pole vault, and two for the broad
jump and hop, step and jump. These measurers shall
be responsible for commenceing their respective events
at such time as may be decided upon by the Executive
Committee on each afternoon of the meet, and for
their continuance without unnecessary delays. They
shall excuse a contestant from a field event in which
he is taking part, for a period long enough to contest
in a heat in a track event, and allow said contestant to
take his missed turn or turns in said field event within
a reasonable time after the track heat. They shall see
that reasonable opportunities are given to contestants
who desire to try in two field events that are being
contested at the same time. To the end that there may
be no unnecessary delay, each competitor shall take
his trial or turn when called upon to so do by the Field

Judge having charge of the contest; and if, in the opinion of such Field Judge, the competitor unreasonably delays to do so, such Judge may, in his discretion, declare such trial forfeit and have the same tallied against the competitor as one miss or failure.

VI.—Time-Keepers.

Each of the three Time-Keepers shall time every event; and in case two watches agree, and the third disagrees, the time marked by the two shall be official time; and if all watches disagree, the time marked by the watch giving the middle time shall be the official time; if there be but two time-keepers, and their watches do not agree, the time marked by the slowest watch shall be the official time. Time shall be taken from the flash of the pistol.

VII.—Clerk of the Course.

The Clerk of the Course shall record the name of each competitor who shall report to him, and shall give him his number for each event in which he is entered, and notify him before the start of every event in which he is engaged. He shall be responsible for getting out at the proper time the contestants for each event.

The assistants shall do such work as he may assign to them.

VIII.—Scorer.

The Scorer shall keep a record of the starters and point winners in each event, together with their respective places. He shall record the laps made by each competitor, and call them aloud, when tallied, for the benefit of the contestants.

The assistants shall do such portions of his work as he may assign to them.

IX.—Starter.

The Starter shall have entire control of the competitors at marks, and shall be the sole judge of fact as to whether or not any man has gone over his mark. He shall be responsible for starting the track events promptly on the afternoon of the meet at such time as the Executive Committee shall direct. He shall also be responsible for any unnecessary delay in the continuance of said events.

X.—Competitors.

Immediately on arriving at the grounds, each competitor shall report to the Clerk of the Course and obtain his number for the game in which he is entered. He shall inform himself of the times at which he must compete, and shall report promptly at the start, without waiting to be notified. No competitor shall be allowed to start without his proper number.

XI.—Protests.

Verbal protests may be made at or before any athletic meeting against a competitor or team, by any competitor or High School competing; but such protest must be subsequently, and before action thereon, made in writing, and duly presented to the Association.

XII.—Inner Grounds.

No person whatever shall be allowed inside the track, except the officials and properly accredited representatives of the press. Authorized persons shall wear a badge. Competitors not engaged in the game actually taking place shall not be allowed inside or upon the track.

XIII.—Track.

The measurements of tracks shall be 12 inches from the inner edge, which edge shall be a solid curb raised three inches above the level of the track.

XIV.—Attendants.

No attendant shall accompany a competitor on the scratch or in the race.

XV.—Starting Signals.

All races (except time handicaps) shall be started by the report of pistol, the pistol to be fired so that its flash may be visible to the Time-Keepers. A snap cap shall be no start. Time handicaps shall be started by the word "Go."

XVI.—Starting.

When the Starter receives a signal from the Judge at the finish that everything is in readiness, he shall direct the competitors to get on their marks. The competitor shall be held to have started when any portion of his body touches the ground in front of his mark. Stations count from the inside.

If in the opinion of the Starter, a false start has been made, he may recall the competitors by a second pistol shot, and penalize the offender or the offenders.

For all races up to and including 125 yards, the competitor shall be put back one yard for the first and another for the second attempt; in races over 125 yards and including 300 yards, two yards for the first and two yards for the second; in races over 300 yards and

including 600 yards, three yards for the first and three
yards for the second; in races over 600 yards, and including 1,000 yards, four yards for the first and four
yards for the second; in races over 1,000 yards and including one mile, five yards for the first and five yards
for the second.

In all cases the third false start shall disqualify the
competitor from the event. In relay races the penalty
shall be according to the distance the offender is to
run in the race.

The Starter must have at least two good cartridges
in his pistol before starting a heat.

XVII.—Keeping Proper Course.

In all races on a straight track each competitor shall
keep his own position on the course from start to finish.
In the 100- and 220-yards dashes, courses for contestants shall be marked on the ground.

XVIII.—Change of Course.

In all races other than on a straight track, a competitor may change toward the inside only when he
is two strides ahead of the man whose path he crosses.

XIX.—Fouling.

Any competitor may be disqualified by the Referee
for jostling, running across, or in any other way impeding another, and all the competitors representing
a High School in any one event may be disqualified by
the Referee by the act of any one of such competitors
in jostling, running across or in any way impeding
another.

XX.—Finish.

The finish line shall be a line on the ground drawn across the track from finish post to finish post, and the men shall be placed in the order in which they completely cross the line. For the purpose of aiding the judges, but not as the finish line, a thread shall be stretched across the track at the finish, four feet above the ground; it shall not be held by the Judges, but fastened to the finish posts on either side so that it may always be at right angles to the course and parallel to the ground; this thread should be "breasted" by the competitor or competitors in finishing and not seized with the hands.

XXI.—Hurdles.

· 120-yards hurdle race shall be over ten hurdles, each three feet six inches high. The first hurdle shall be placed 15 yards from the scratch, and there shall be ten yards between each hurdle. 220-yards hurdle race shall be over ten hurdles, each two feet six inches high. The first hurdle shall be placed 20 yards from the scratc' and there shall be 20 yards between each hurdle. No record shall be made in a hurdle race unless each of the hurdles, at the time the competitor jumps the same, is standing, and is not knocked down by such competitor.

A competitor knocking down three or more hurdles, or any portion of three or more hurdles in a race shall be disqualified. A competitor who trails his leg or foot alongside any hurdle shall be disqualified.

XXII.—Jumping.

No weights or artificial aid will be allowed in any jumping contest except by special agreement or announcement. When weights are allowed, there shall be no restrictions as to size, shape or material.

XXIII.—Running High Jump and Pole-Vault.

The height of the bar at starting and at each successive elevation shall be determined by the measurers. Three tries allowed at each height. Each competitor shall make one attempt in the order of his name on the programme; then those who have failed (if any) shall have a second trial in regular order, and those failing on this trial shall take their final trial. A competitor may omit his trials at any height, but if he fail at the next height he shall not be allowed to go back and try the height he omitted. Each competitor shall be credited with the best of all his jumps or vaults.

High Jump.—A line shall be drawn three feet in front of the bar and parallel therewith, and stepping over such a line, to be known as the balk line, in any attempt, shall count as a balk. Three balks shall count as a "try." Displacing the bar shall count as a "try."

Pole Vault.—A line shall be drawn 15 feet in fr⸱ of the bar and parallel therewith, and stepping over such line, to be known as the balk line, in any attempt, shall count as a balk. Two balks shall count as a "try." Displacing the bar or leaving the ground in an attempt shall count as a "try." The poles shall be unlimited as to size and weight, but shall have no assistant device, except that they may be wound or wrapped with any substance for the purpose of affording a firmer grasp, and may have one prong at the lower end.

No competitor shall, during his vault, raise the hand which was uppermost when he left the ground to a higher point on the pole, nor shall he raise the hand which was undermost when he left the ground to any point on the pole above the other hand.

Any competitor shall be allowed to dig a hole not more than one foot in diameter at the take-off in which to plant his pole.

XXIV.—Running Broad Jump.

The competitors shall have unlimited run, but must take off from or behind the scratch line. The scratch line shall be the outer edge of a joint eight inches wide; which shall be set firmly in and be on the same level as the ground; the earth in front of this joint may, however, be removed to the depth of not more than one-half inch and the width of not more than six inches. When any part of the competitor's foot is over the scratch line, while taking off for a jump, it shall be no jump, but shall, however, count as a ''try.'' Each competitor shall be allowed three trials, and the best four men shall have three more trials each. Each competitor shall be credited with the best of his jumps. The measurement shall be from the outer edge of the joist to the nearest break of the ground made by any part of his person. A line shall be drawn six feet in front of the scratch line, and stepping over such line in an attempt shall count as a balk; three balks count as a ''try.''

XXV.—Putting the Shot.

The shot shall be a metal sphere weighing 12 pounds. It shall be put from the shoulder with each hand, and during the attempt it shall not pass behind nor below the shoulder. It shall be put from a circle seven feet in diameter, four feet of whose circumference shall be a toe board, four inches in height. Foul puts, which shall not be measured, but which shall count as puts, are as follows:

1. Letting go of the shot in an attempt.

2. Touching the ground outside the circle with any portion of the body while the shot is in hand.

3. Touching the ground forward on the front half of the circle with any portion of the body before the put is measured.

Each competitor shall be allowed three puts, and the best four men shall each be allowed three more puts. Each competitor shall be credited with the best of all his puts. The measurement of the put shall be from the nearest edge of the first mark made by the shot to the point of the circumference of the circle nearest such mark.

XXVI.—Throwing the Hammer.

The hammer shall be a metal sphere, and the handle shall be made of wire. Such wire must be the best grade spring steel wire, not less than one-eighth of an inch in diameter; or, No. 36 piano wire, the diameter of which is 102-1000 of an inch. If a loop grip is used, it must be of rigid construction. The length of the complete implement shall be not more than four feet, and its weight not less than 12 pounds.

The hammer shall be thrown from a circle seven feet in diameter. In making an attempt a competitor may assume any position he pleases. Foul throws, which shall not be measured but which shall count as throws, are as follows:

1. Letting go of the hammer in an attempt.

2. Touching the ground outside the circle with

any portion of the body while the hammer is in hand.

3. Touching the ground forward of the front half of the circle with any portion of the body before the throw is measured.

Each competitor shall be allowed three throws, and the best four men shall each be allowed three more throws. Each competitor shall be credited with the best of all his throws. The measurement of the throw shall be from the nearest edge of the first mark made by the head of the hammer to the point of the circumference of the circle nearest such mark.

XXVII.—Running, Hop, Step, and Jump.

The competitor shall first land upon the same foot with which he shall have taken off. The reverse foot shall be used for the second landing, and both feet shall be used for the third landing.

In all other respects the rules governing the Running Broad Jump shall also govern the Running Hop, Step, and Jump.

XXVIII.—Relay Race.

A line shall be drawn ten yards on each side of the starting line of each relay, the space between these lines to be known as the starting zone. Within this zone each runner must touch the succeeding runner. No member of a relay team, in order to relieve his team-mat, may run outside of this zone. The position of the teams shall be drawn for.

New Mexico Interscholastic Records.

Event	Time	Holder	School	Year
100-yards Dash	10 1-5 Sec.	Smaulding	Albuquerque H.S.	1916
220-yards Dash	23 3-5 Sec.	Smaulding	Albuquerque H.S.	1916
120-yards High Hurdle	17 3-5 Sec.	Smaulding	Albuquerque H.S.	1916
220-yards Low Hurdle	27 4-5 Sec.	Hill	Roswell H. S.	1916
440-yards Run	56 Sec.	Johnson	Roswell H. S.	1916
Half Mile Run	2 Min. 12 Sec.	Johnson	Roswell H. S.	1916
One Mile Run	5 M. 12 Sec.	Kremis	Albuquerque H.S.	1916
Running High Jump	5 ft. 7 3-4 in.	Wohlenberg	Alamogordo H.S.	1916
Running Broad Jump	21 ft. 1-2 in.	Evans	Albuquerque H.S.	1916
Running Hop, Step & Jump	42 ft. 1 1-5 in.	Arnold	Roswell H. S.	1915
Pole Vault	10 ft. 2 3-4 in.	Smaulding	Albuquerque H.S.	1916
Putting 12lb. Shot	41 ft. 8 2-5 in.	Higgins	Roswell H. S.	1915
Relay Race	3 Min. 55 2-5 Sec.		Roswell H. S.	1916

The Basketball Tournament.

I. Rules. All games will be played according to the Official Basketball Rules of the current· season.

II. The Tournament will be conducted as an elimination contest, the order in which the teams are to play being decided by lot. The team which is undefeated at the end of the tournament will be declared the Champion, and will be entitled to the Tournament Cup.

III. Any High School which is a member of the Association may enter a team in this tournament. No preliminary sectional contests are required.

IV. No more than nine men may be entered for positions on any one team.

V. All entries must be made on the ,official blanks and returned to the committee before Tuesday, April 24.

The Oratorical and Declamatory Contest.

I. Rules (extracts from Constitution) :

"11. The contest features shall be orations for boys and declamations for girls.

"12· In the oratorical contest the orations may be either original or selected.

"13· The lyceum contestant who exceeds fifteen minutes in delivery shall be given no award of place or honor.

"14· Three or five judges shall be chosen by, the State Board of Control to judge the contests and each school interested shall be notified of their appointment at least three weeks before the time of the ,contest.

"15. The judges shall not be from the same city or any school represented in the contest. This rule, however, shall not apply to members of the faculty of the University of New Mexico.

"16· Any judge may be removed upon the written protest of any school represented, provided no school shall be allowed more than two protests."

II. The state is divided into five districts (see under Lyceum Districts, page 39) for the purpose of conducting preliminary contests.

III. The winners of these district contests are eligible to compete in the state contest.   .

IV. In case it has been impossible to hold a preliminary contest in any section, that district may be represented in the state contest by one orator and one declaimer. In case of the receipt of entry blanks for more than one orator or more than one declaimer from such a district, the first entry received will be accepted and all others returned.

V. All entries must be made on the official entry blank, and must be accompanied by a statement from the district secretary to the effect that the entrant was awarded first place in the district contest.

For particulars in regard to the district contests, see the Constitution, and write to the President or the Secretary of the Association for the names of your section officers, etc.

The New Mexico High School Athletic and Lyceum Association.

OFFICERS.

E. C. Ringer, Santa Fe....................President
E. V. Wiseman, Santa Rosa...........Vice-President
Ruth Clark, Raton...............Secretary-Treasurer

BOARD OF CONTROL.

Andrew McCurdy, Carrizozo; W. D. Shadwick, Tucumcari; A. R. Kent, Raton

CONSTITUTION.

Administration.

Section 1.—The officers shall be a President, a Vice President, and a Secretary-Treasurer. The duties of these officers shall be the usual duties devolving upon such officers.

Sec. 2. A Board of Control, composed of three members, who shall be high school principals or superintendents, shall be elected by this Association on Wednesday preceding Thanksgiving, 1915, as follows: One for one year, one for two years, and one for three years, the chairman each year to be the one whose term expires at the end of that year. Thereafter, each member of the Board shall be elected for three years. This election is to take place at the annual meeting of the New Mexico Educational Association. In case of vacancy the remaining members of the Board may appoint a person to fill the vacancy until the next annual meeting of the Association.

Sec. 3. Each newly elected member of the Board of control shall assume the duties of his office on the first day of Jannary next following.

Sec. 4. No retiring member of the Board of Control, having served three years, shall be eligible for service on that Board for a period of one year after date of retirement.

Sec. 5. The Board of Control shall have the following powers and duties: (a) It shall have general control over all athletic and declamatory contests between secondary schools of this Association. (b) The annual Interscholastic Track Meet, Basket Ball Tournament, and Oratorical and Declamatory Contest shall be held under the auspices of the University of New Mexico, but the rules that govern it shall be made by the Board of Control of this Association. (c) It shall give interpretations to the rules of the Association. (d) It shall determine forfeitures under Sec. 13. (e) The Board of Control, at the end of any athletic season may, at its discretion, issue a statement of its official opinion as to the relative standing of teams. No school which has violated the rules of the Association in regard to the qualifications of players shall be awarded special honors in that particular branch of athletics.

Sec. 6. (a) When charges are made in writing by a member of the Association against another member for violation of the rules of the Association, the Board of Control, after giving due notice of the place and time for the school so charged to be heard, shall consider such charges, and may suspend the offending school for a period of not exceeding one year. (b) The

Board of Control shall decide on all protests brought before it with reference to qualifications of contestants in the Interscholastic meet. (c) When any matter comes before the Board for decision which is of special interest to a school of which a member is a representative, it shall appoint another member to act in his place in that matter.

Sec. 7. The Secretary-Treasurer shall have charge of the property and records of the Association; shall receive all money for dues and the sale of publications of the Association; shall issue all circulars authorized by the Board of Control; shall attend meetings of the Board when requested to do so by the Board; shall turn over to the Treasurer of the Board all moneys in his possession when called upon to do so; shall perform such other duties as the growth of the Association as determined by the Board may require; and shall receive such allowance for expenses as the Board may approve. Vacancies in the office may be declared by the Board for cause, and a successor may be appointed by the Board to act until the next annual meeting.

Local Management.

Sec. 8. The Principal or his authorized representative shall accompany his team to all contests.

Sec. 9. The Principal of the High School, or high school teachers authorized by him, shall be manager or managers of teams representing the school.

Sec. 10. No games shall be played or cancelled without the sanction of the Principal or Superintendent.

Sec. 11. The eligibility of all contestants shall be certified by the Principal or Superintendent of the

School in accordance with the rules hereby adopted. Such statements shall be presented in writing within three days before any contest. In case of disputes the principal must furnish the Board of Control the following data in regard to each contestant: The date of last enrollment; the date and place of birth; average mark in each study for the last preceding term in school; average in each study from the beginning of the current term or semester. A school which does not furnish this data shall be denied championship honors and may be excluded from the annual Interscholastic Meet.

Sec. 12. The Principal shall have power and is advised to exclude any contestant who, because of bad habits or improper conduct, would not represent his school in a becoming manner.

Sec. 13. It is recommended that Principals, in arranging for games, provide a forfeit to be exacted should there be a failure on the part of either party to carry out the arrangements made. Should such forfeiture be stipulated and not paid during the same season, the Board of Control, after hearing both sides, shall have authority to expel the delinquent school from the Association. Notification of such expulsion shall be published in the papers, with cause therefor.

Sec. 14. Paid coaches, other than those regularly employed as teachers by the trustees of the school, are prohibited. By paid coaches is meant any person who receives, directly or indirectly, remuneration of any kind in return for services rendered in instructing or coaching high school teams. Necessary traveling expenses shall not be construed as remuneration.

Sec. 15. Each school in the Association shall report to the Secretary a list of the pupils representing the school in contests during the year. Each school is asked to report also the kind of treatment accorded them, from and on the field, while at another school.

Athletic Officials.

.Sec. 16. On and after January 1, 1916, all the major officials in all athletic contests participated in by teams connected with schools in this Association shall be regularly licensed teachers in the public schools of New Mexico or shall be persons whose names have been furnished and approved by the managers of the contesting teams. It is recommended that these officials shall be disinterested, and it is required that when a school demands disinterested officials at the time of scheduling the game, such officials shall be furnished. The Board shall drop from its list of approved officials any person who is palpably unfair and biased in his decision in games.

Sec. 17. Non-playing students, officials, or assistants conform to the same rules as the players.

Membership.

Sec. 18. Membership in this Association shall be limited to public high schools in the state, and each school shall have one vote. The annual dues shall be payable when the school becomes a member, and thereafter by December 1 of each year, in advance. Secondary schools, that is, schools doing work between the Eighth grade and College or University, shall be eligible to membership in the Association and whereve' the words High School appear in this Constitution it shall be understood to apply equally to these secondary schools.

Sec. 19.   No game shall be played with high schools of this state not belonging to this Association.

This rule does not prevent a member of the Association from playing high school teams outside of the state, nor from playing non-high school teams within the state, except as follows:

It is a violation of the Constitution for schools in the Association to play non-high school teams including high school boys, unless the latter are certified as eligible by the Principal of the school to which they belong.

Sec. 20.   The games recognized by this Association shall be: Football, Rugby Football, Soccer, Basketball, Track Work, Baseball, Tennis, and Girls' Basketball. Further all forms of inter-school athletic games shall be subject to the rules of the N. M. H. S. A. & L. A.

Sec. 21.   The number of interscholastic football games played by any team in one season is limited to six.

Sec. 22.   In all football contests held under these rules, the length of each quarter shall be fifteen minutes, unless changed by mutual consent.

Sec. 23.   The Basketball rules as published in Spalding's Official Basketball Rule Book shall be the official rules. Rules governing the selection of officials in the above rules shall be void and unless otherwise agreed by mutual consent, each school shall furnish one major official, and these officials shall alternate their duties, each acting as umpire during one half.

RULES.

Eligibility.

Rule 1. To represent a school in any interscholastic contest the contestant must be under twenty-one years of age except by mutual consent, must have entered some public high school within the first twenty school days of the semester in which the contest occurs, and must be an amateur as defined by the A. A. U. A semester is one-half of the school year.

The term "Amateur" is defined and fully explained on pages 80 and 160 of Spalding's "Official Y. M. C. A. Athletic League Handbook."

Rule 2. A pupil withdrawing permanently from school within the first twenty school days of the semester shall not be regarded as having had an opportunity to engage in athletics for that semester unless he has already played in one or more interscholastic games, in which case he shall be regarded as having engaged in athletics for that season.

Rule 3. Post-graduates are not eligible to enter athletic or declamatory contests, but pupils graduating from regular three-year courses shall not be deemed post-graduates.

Rule 4. A student is a post-graduate of a school after he has completed the work required for graduation by that school, irrespective of the time of granting the diploma.

Rule 5. Time spent in athletic sport by pupils while in the grades below the high school shall not be counted as a part of the four years.

Rule 6. No person shall enter a contest under an assumed name.

Rule 7.   Any member of a high school athletic team who participates in an athletic contest as a member of any other similar team the same season, shall be eligible to compete under these rules for the remainder of that season.

An exception is hereby made for basketball and basketball players in those towns and cities whose schools have no gymnasium and whose students are forced by necessity to use a Y. M. C. A. or some other gymnasium for their practice games.   It is a well-known fact that the use of such gymnasium by high school students under such circumstances will likely require that such students play on the teams of the organization maintaining such gymnasiums.   No student, however, will be allowed to play on any other teams without the knowledge and consent of his Principal.

Rule 8.   Each contestant must have and be maintaining for the current semester, a passing grade in each of three or more studies requiring a minimum of fifteen regular high school recitations per week exclusive of rhetoricals, physical culture, military drill and deportment.   In his last preceding semester in school he must also have met the same requirements throughout the entire term.

Pupils enrolling for the first time must comply with the requirements of the rules, the average standing required for the preceding semester being obtained from the records in the last secondary school attended.

Back work may be made up, providing it be done in accordance with the regular rules of the school and become a matter of final record before the next semester.

Interpretations: In each of the studies represented as the minimum requirements of work specified above: (a) for the current semester the average of the monthly grades up to the time of certification must be passing; (b) for the current school month the average of the daily or weekly grades must be passing; (c) if the average of the monthly grades at the beginning of any month is below passing in any study, the pupil is ineligible so far as that study is concerned for the entire month.

Rule 9. No person who has been enrolled as a student in an institution of college standing and has done work which may be counted toward a degree in that institution, shall be eligible as a member of any athletic team under these rules in any game with any other team, either within or without the state of New Mexico.

Rule 10. The eligibility rules of this Association shall apply to students taking part in all contests, whether with schools inside or outside of the state of New Mexico.

Rules for Lyceum Work.

Rule 11. The contest features shall be orations for boys and declamations for girls.

Rule 12. In the oratorical contest the orations may be either original or selected.

Rule 13. The lyceum contestant who exceeds fifteen minutes in delivery shall be given no award of place or honor.

Rule 14· Three or five judges shall be chosen by the State Board of Control to judge the contests and each school interested shall be notified of their appointment at least three weeks before the time of the contest.

Rule 15. The judges shall not be from the same city or any school represented in the contest. This rule, however, shall not apply to members of the faculty of the University of New Mexico.

Rule 16. Any judge may be removed upon the written protest of any school represented, provided no school shall be allowed more than two protests.

Rule 17. All markings shall be on the scale of one hundred per cent. No grade shall be below seventy per cent, and no judge shall mark any two contestants alike.

Rule 18. At the close of the contest the President and Secretary shall take the grades of all the judges for each contestant. The grades of each judge shall be ranked 1, 2, 3, etc. The contestant ranked first by a majority of the judges shall be awarded first place. If no contestant is thus ranked first, the contestant the sum of whose ranks is least shall be awarded first place. In case of a tie the contestant receiving the highest grand average in per cent shall be awarded first place. The other places shall be awarded in like manner.

INTERPRETATIONS.

First. A game is any athletic contest where an admission fee is charged, or where any collection or contribution is received from spectators.

Second. The football season is defined as beginning with the opening of school and closing with November 30.

Third. No student who violates the rules of the

Association will be reinstated by the Board for one year from date of violation.

Fourth. A pupil who has played in one or more interscholastic games in any season shall be regarded as having engaged in athletics for that season.

Fifth. When a member or members of any team are protested, the game should be played as scheduled and the protest filed with the Board for settlement later.

Sixth. By mutual consent of both teams, pupils over the age of twenty-one may be allowed to enter a contest played under these rules.

Seventh. Pupils under the age of twenty-one at the time of registration in school shall be so regarded until the time of their next registration.

Eighth. Any student who carries at least fifteen hours of regular high school work, is a high school student.

LYCEUM DISTRICTS.

For the purpose of high school lyceum contests the State of New Mexico shall be divided into five districts as follows:

1. District No. 1 to include the counties of San Juan, Rio Arriba, Taos, McKinley, Sandoval, Santa Fe, Valencia, Bernalillo, and Torrance.

2. District No. 2 to include the counties of Colfax, Mora, Union, and San Miguel.

3. District No. 3 to include the counties of Quay, Guadalupe, Curry, and Roosevelt.

4. District No. 4 to include the counties of Socorro, Sierra, Grant, Luna, Dona Ana, and Otero.

5.   District No. 5 to include the counties of Chaves,. Eddy, and Lincoln.

The officers of each district shall be a President, a Vice-President, and a Secretary-Treasurer.

Each District shall make its own rules and regulations with reference to local matters within the district, but the general rules of this Constitution shall be observed by the districts.

Each district shall be represented at the state contest by one orator and one declaimer.

The district contests shall be held not later than three weeks before the state contest, and the Secretary-Treasurer of the district shall within one week after the contest, make a report to the Secretary-Treasurer of the State Association indicating the winner of first and of second place in oratory and in declamation.

NOTE.

All correspondence and remittances from members of the Association to the Board of Control or to the Secretray must be endorsed by the Principal or a member of the faculty.

AMENDMENTS.

This Constitution may be amended by a majority vote of the schools represented at the annual meeting to be held at the time and place of the annual meeting of the New Mexico Educational Association.

Local Managing Committees.

UNIVERSITY OF NEW MEXICO.

The Track and Field Meet.

A. O. Weese.....President Athletic Council, Chairman

D. R. Boyd...................President of the University

R. F. Hutchinson.....................Physical Director

_____..........Manager Track Team

_____..........Captain Track Team

The Basketball Tournament.

A. O. Weese.....President Athletic Council, Chairman

D. R. Boyd...................President of the University

R. F. Hutchonsin..................Physical Director

Floyd Lee...............Manager Basketball Team

Ray McCanna...............Captain Basketball Team

The Oratorical and Declamatory Contest.

D. A. Worcester...............................

..........Chairman Oratorical and Debate Committee

D. R. Boyd...............President of the University

C. E. Bonnett

R. R. Hill

Carl Brorein...............Member Oratorical Squad

Lightning Source UK Ltd.
Milton Keynes UK
UKHW011850140219
337178UK00015B/168/P

9 780428 149628